Katarzyna Dorosz

Your path to happiness

Health with absolutely no age limits

I dedicate this book to Mrs. Alicja Bielenia

*– Some people make the world special,
just because they are in it.*

Our body is incredible – Imagine a powerful and comprehensive machine where every single component, even the smallest part has its own task and responsibility.

Is our everyday diet and lifestyle affecting our happiness and ultimately ourselves? Do we really have full control over our health, emotions, and psyche? These are only a few of the questions that we will be pursued in this book. Let's be honest, even a 1000-page book wouldn't be enough to fully elaborate or discuss these problems. However, we need to adapt to our fast pace of living and the constant lack of spare time that limits our ability to care for ourselves. This book is designed for your busy lifestyle. It will answer the most important questions for you in a time-efficient manner.

Why people are hurting themselves so badly?

This question is unbelievably easy to answer. Failure of good routines in both private and professional life, bad eating habits etc.. Nobody „celebrates" meals anymore, as we did in the past as a family. Today, we're treating eating like just another thing to do in our busy lives. We do not know, or care what we are eating or how to eat it properly – we just eat to fight hunger, not to help our body work for us properly, and stay healthy. It's not just about how we care for ourselves. We have forgotten how to treat our body like a temple and celebrate health every day. Surely as human beings, we deserve the best.

Often, it doesn't really matter if our meal is fancy – it's the joy and satisfaction that comes with serving an amazing meal that really counts. Simple things count sometimes: elegant dinnerware, a candle, beautiful napkins. It all matters because it changes your inner peace and satisfaction with life. Moreover, it's the key to understanding the way in which our body (and soul) "digests" a meal.

You are probably meticulous in caring about the maintenance of your car – no doubt you use high quality gas, perform regular maintenance and service checks etc. If you even suspect that something may be wrong do you not go immediately to see a mechanic. Would you afford your body even a fraction of the same care?

It's unbelievable how people in the 21st century, living in the so-called developed world and possesing all the opportunities to care for our body well, are self-destructing their health through negligence – constant rush, stress, inactivity and bad diet. People in less developed countries are forced to live differently and keep better life-style habits. Is this an inevitable cost of social development? It seems to be a little bit too high.

You are what you eat

Every single cell in our body needs different biological nutrients. Your job is to make sure you're providing them. It's the best way to make sure your body stays in good health for longer. Wouldn't it be nice to stand in front of the mirror every day and be able to honestly say: "I'm caring about myself, because I love myself".

It's a simple truth - as long as one cannot love and accept oneself, one cannot truly love anybody else.

This book is for anyone who wants to live in harmony with themselves and nature. If you want to discover the simplest joy of life in large and little things – this book is right for you. You will learn how to extract immense happiness from even the small things that grace our everyday lives, stay healthy, and care about yourself.

I hope that these few simple but profound suggestions will lead you to making a seminal change in your life and become a happier more fulfilled person.

Because our breath
connects our mind with our body
by building a bridge
between the conscious and the unconscious,
Today I will direct my attention every given moment
towards my breath.
This is how I will face
the present.

Chapter 1

Body and psyche

Everything starts in your "head" – because
the mind determines how your emotions
and beliefs affect your health.

It's not a new discovery, in fact it's rather more than common knowledge that our emotions and mental state have a crucial impact on our physical health. How often have you heard the phrase: "scared to death" or "it broke my heart"? These common sayings are not that far from reality...

Modern, scientists have proved many times over, that there is an important relation between mental and physical health. However, the belief that a sudden emotional breakdown can cause death goes all the way back to biblical times. Medical science has shown us that a sudden high level of fear can lead to sudden death. This is not an uncommon occurrence nowadays. After an earthquake in 1994, doctors from Good Samaritan Hospital Los Angeles studied the incidence of heart attacks and sudden death. The results presented to the American College of Cardiology were unambiguous – on the day of the earthquake, the rate of deaths caused by heart attack was suddenly and significantly higher.

The mind-body connection seems an easy proof but it's worth stopping for a minute, and thinking about this relationship between body and mind. You should actually regard the mind-body axis as a single united "mechanism". The problem is, that today many people have ignored it. As long as we or somebone close to us, is not facing serious health problems, we have chosen to ignored these issues. Too often in modern reality, time for self-health caring is replaced by time for earning more money or spending it.

Consumer lifestyle disadvantages

Where is the time for relaxation or vacation? Time without the siren calls of the ever demanding cell phone? We're living with constant stress, instantaneous decision making, and mounting responsibilities. This lifestyle impacts negatively on our mental health, our emotions, self-esteem and perception.

Psychologist - Lidia Temoshok published research proving clearly that the systematic pursuit of poor lifestyle habits can cause the development and progression of cancer. She called it a "type C personality". Characteristic features of this kind of type C personality are a tendency to sacrifice, excessive affability or submissiveness, idle stress reactions, and the extinguishing of anger and negative emotions. Temoshok presents the task of stress facing methods as a continuum. In her opinion, people with the biggest chances to develop cancer are the ones that would be commonly regarded as "the kindest of all". It appears the meek do not necessarily always inherit the world.

Be assertive, don't hide your anger!

How to we fight the stress? Work it out! Be active – swim, run, take yoga classes. Personally, I would recommend flamenco to dance the stress out vigorously and rhythmically.

Don't hide your emotions – especially the negative ones. Never let them accumulate and fester. In the evening, instead of watching TV, go outside and take a walk, calm down, slow down, take a few minutes to contemplate nature, the sun, the moon, stars, wind, maybe just birdsong. Do something special for yourself, now – not later when it's too late. Above all, take care of and love yourself just the same way you care for love your family, friends, pets, career, or car.

How the mind can affect the body: Psychoneuroimmunology

In 1981, Robert Ader by releasing his new book - "Psychoneuroim-munology" founded a brand-new field in psychology. He was writing about connections between the immune system and the brain, and its impact on overall human health. He named the important connections between three human body systems – the immune, endocrine and nervous systems. At the time this was a revolutionary concept in medicine.

The immune system is made up of many types of cells and organs working together to defend the body against negative "attacks" from the outside environment. When everything works well, the immune system is fighting against many pathogens like viruses and bacteria. Sometimes, the system malfunctions and falsely recognizes some neutral body antigens as pathogens and turns against itself causing serious disease called "auto-immune" disease.

How the immune system works

The immune system plays a crucial role in the fight against cancer. One scientific theory proposes that normally immune cells are constantly "patrolling" the body to find and destroy potential cancer cells. It follows therefore that if the immune system is overworked, or malfunctioning, it may give rise to the emergence of cancer. The immune system is an indispensable weapon against cancer made out of many different types of immune cells.

Here we present just a few of them:

Lymphocytes: These are white blood cells, and the most important elements of the immune system. There are two basic types of lymphocytes – B-cells and T-cells.

B Lymphocytes (B Cells): These are responsible for secreting antibodies against antigens. Antigens are the molecular components on the surface of viruses, bacteria and other pathogens that circulate in the bloodstream. B-cells have the capacity to recognize antigen to fight against a particular type of pathogen.

T Lymphocytes (killer T cell) –it's the kind of lymphocytes that regulates immune reactions. T cells produce cytokines, kind of protein that stimulates other cells to defend the body from pathogens. T cells fight directly only with one kind of pathogen. It can attack cancer cells. There are two kinds of T cells.

T helper cells – essential for activating B and T cells and other immunological reactions. Significant deficiency of T helper cells is characteristic for people struggling with AIDS. Helper-T-cell activation help activate cytotoxic T cells and macrophages to attack infected cells, or they stimulate B cells to secrete antibodies.

Suppressor T cells (regulatory T cells) – responsible for "turning off" helper cells after they produce enough antigens to prevent the body from the autoimmune disease.

Natural Killer Cells (NK Cells) – critical immunity weapon. They are different from T cells – they don't need to recognize the antigen kind. It's important for fighting many kinds of pathogens.

Phagocyte –white blood cells with the ability to engulf and remove the bacteria and other pathogens from blood.

Macrophages – specific type of phagocyte, universally present. It engulfs the microbes and antigens once activated by the immune system.

The immune system incorporates many organs like bone marrow, thymus, lymph node, spleen, tonsils, lymphatic and blood vessels.

Psychoneuroimmunology (PNI) tells us about the connections between psychological aspects and interactions in function of the neurologic and endocrine systems, with immune processes. It describes how these three "areas" commonlyy interact to affect our health.

Here you have some examples of new research areas of this incredibly interesting field of science:
- Effect of brain damage may affect the immune system,
- Laterality (dominance of one side of the brain over the other in controlling key functions) and its impact on immune system diseases,
- Factors that boost the immune system to fight pathogens.

Stress and relaxation

Every one of us sometimes feels extreme tiredness caused by too many hours of work in a row. Every year in Japan over 30,000 people die from overwork. American economist – Juliet B with her research proved that every generation of Americans *loses* 47 hours of free time compared to the previous generation. In 1886, science reached the conclusion that stress is a disease, not caused by what happens to people, but by how they react to these situations.

The term "stress" was first used by Hans Hugon Selye, who focused his entire 50 years of scientific career on this phenomenon. He published over 1400 articles, and 30 books just about stress! After all these years his friends even gave him a nickname – Dr. Stress.

Seleye was the first who came up with the idea that many somatic diseases are in fact caused by problems in dealing with anger and stress. In his first book, **The stress of life,** he introduced the term of General Adaptation Syndrome (GAS), and how problems with it may cause many serious health issues. In his work, he often referred to the principles of Walter Cannon.

Walter Cannon is called the father of the philosophy of stress. Based on the work of 19th-century French philosopher and physiologist, Claude Bernard, he established the term *homeostasis*. In his book, *The winsome of the body,* he showed how the human body naturally attunes to pursuing, attaining, and preserving the internal balance of the body ("le milieu intérieur" of Bernard) as a reaction to the external environmental factors. This natural balance was what he called *homeostasis*.

Cannon brought the "fight or flight response" theory to popular understanding. It shows the two opposite ways that people react to stress. In ancient times, people faced different stressors, for example, natural disasters or attacking predators, nowadays – we're struggling with a stressful job, societal pressure, money issues, and even problems in family and private life…"plus ça change, plus c'est la même chose".

When something is frightening you, your sympathetic system jolts into action. Your body produces catecholamines – the kind of hormones that pushes all organs to react maximally to the stressful situation. After only a few seconds adrenaline and noradrenaline is released which then quickly elicits significant changes in the entire body. Your heart beats way faster, the breathing is quicker and shallower, and the blood pressure and blood sugar levels are instantly rising. Visual perception is enhanced and at the same time, the perception of pain decreases. The digestive system temporarily stops working - together with all processes responsible for growing and reproduction. Priorities are reassigned to stress reactions.

Based on Cannon's work, Selye proved that the lack of emotional and psychological harmony may cause serious physical disease. What is important to understand, he also reiterated is that *not every stress is bad*, and *not every stress causes harm*. Short, controlled, and not too intense stress may positively affect both intellectual and emotional development.

From the medical point of view, stress is a natural process and is causing many specific whole-body changes. Also, not only humans but also animals experience this.

Stress may be caused by psychological stimulants, like internal or external conflicts either with another person or frustration within oneself. However, there are also some biological factors that may bring about the same effect, for example, extreme temperatures, or physical stress from exertion, hunger or pain.

Stress can be divided into three stages:
– alarm reaction,
– resistance,
– exhaustion.

Stress causes disturbance of internal homeostasis. In some cases, when the stress reaction is extremely intense, it may cause the exhaustion of abilities to adapt and fight back, what can lead to many health problems like circulatory diseases, rheumatism, digestive and metabolic disturbances, or even allergic skin reactions.

Relaxation

Commonly, relaxation is associated with physical and emotional respite and relief. More professionally, it would be called as an emotional state of low psychological tension. The term "relaxation" was first used by a physician at Harvard University – Professor Herbert Benson had been working on the meditation research.

Relaxation as an opposition to "fight or flight" response consists of lowered activity of the sympathetic system. For the body it means:
– 10 to 20% lower use of oxygen,
– Slowing of the pulse (about 3 beats per minute less than average),
– Slower and deeper breathing,
– Lower level of lactic acid production,
– Increased production of brain alpha waves.

During the normal day, your brain mostly uses beta waves. When you are relaxing, the frequency of brainwaves lowers, causing lower tension throughout the body. Alpha waves dominate and it's leading to healthier (slower) functioning of all the living processes. It also results in a lower level of stress hormones. In this state a person is more open to suggestions, positive affirmations, and emotions. This so-called "alpha" stage naturally appears right before we fall asleep, and just after waking up.

In addition, relaxation also results in:
– lower tension in the muscles,
– a slower pace of metabolism,
– relaxation and dilation of blood vessels,
– increasing body temperature.

It's important to remember, that during the relaxation your body is loosening all the unneeded muscle tension and leads to muting of the emotions and an overall calming sensation.

According to Benson, relaxation can be achieved with many techniques. Which one is most effective in bringing the best effects always depends one's nature and personal choice. However, no matter which one is chosen, it should be used every day, at least for 10-20 minutes. You should also take care to find a calm and quiet environment, with no distractions.

I think that it's worth mentioning here some research about using prayer as a therapy technique. Benson found many examples, when a Christian *Jesus Prayer* was used as a "relaxation" technique in the 14th-Century Greece. Potential patient were asked to sit still and repeat the words of prayer keeping a rhythmic, calm breathing throughout this process.

To summarize, in any relaxation technique, it's important to:
– systematically repeat sessions at similar time frames,
– choose a place without distractions, calm and quiet, with the presence of some inspirational and/or religious icon or symbol.

This technique helps one to reach a state of total peace and stillness of mind and at the same time concentration. It is evidently true that meditation is a way to still the mind in order to realize the Self within us.

Both in medicine and psychology, doctors are using relaxation techniques as a part of therapy. Proof exists, that relaxation may be very effective in reducing the symptoms of many diverse medical problems and, of course, decreased negative psychological and emotional side effects.

These activities have also been used to activate the immune system, or to bring back homeostasis after allergic or asthma attacks. Having an allergy doesn't mean that the patient's body has a weak immune system, but in fact that the system is "overreacting" to external allergens or pathogens.

All relaxation activities are based on stimulating the parasympathetic nervous system – especially the parts responsible for resting and regeneration. A relaxed body means a lower stress level. How do we recognize this state? Sometimes, you can easily see and feel it – rested muscles, lighter sweating, slower deeper breath. Other effects are no as obvious - lower ratio of stress hormones – cortisol, epinephrine, higher body temperature, and a better blood supply.

Relaxation, as "psychological" training, has a crucial impact not only on our body but also our mind. It lets you control and change the way you're reacting to various psychological states of mind. Thanks to this kind of training you can significantly decrease the chances of experiencing fear and depression, and learn how to control your anger. It can also help you to improve your ability to concentrate.

Visualization

Visualization is simply creating "pictures" in your mind. It consists of imagining things that may be experienced by senses – vision, hearing, taste, smell, and touch. It represents a psychological exercise that helps with motivation, realization of goals, and improving life satisfaction.

Let's learn how to work with your imagination by focusing your mind on a *positive* picture of your necessities and desires. This particular mental picture helps what you really want to become a reality. It only awaits your decision about what you want and how you are going to visualize it.

The main goal here is to change your attitude by changing your thoughts and beliefs. To be the master of your own life and destiny, you will first need to learn how to fully control your mind. Master the MIND-BODY connection!

Your attitude and way of thinking about life is crucial to what is really happening to you. We are doing it all the time – we are controlling our lives totally unconsciously. Every area of your life is affected by the rule of "like attracts like". Positive thinking has positive benefits and vice-versa.

Internal peace and living in self-harmony is the key to understanding all of one's life experiences (both good and bad) which are the sum and effect of one's own thoughts and attitudes. It is you yourself, who is responsible for creating your own reality. Nothing and nobody else matters. With a little help from your mind, you can be Your Creator. Nothing is truly impossible IF you really want it. You should change your desires into the destiny of your will. Then, it becomes easier – will is the intention, this intention becomes the driver, and a goal is whatever is *your choice*.

You should adopt this positive attitude as your default state of mind – part of your everyday life and every session of visualization. This can bring you real peace of mind, the like of which, you have never experienced before. I urge you to take command and full responsibility for your life. This will give you the power to change it for your benefit and that of others.

Psychologist, Jeanne Achterberg from San Francisco, proposed that every society has its own rituals that help its members to face the most difficult moments in their lives. Another scientist – Carl Simonton wrote a book about the role of visualization in fighting cancer – *Getting Well Again.*

**Remember, that visualization should be an addition
to traditional medical therapy, not its substitute!!**

For patients with somatic diseases visualization is used to push the body to fight the illness. It's important to realize that development of illness and the "surrender" in the mental fight against it is happening at the same time both physically and mentally. Scientists are testing the phenomena of a feedback loop that operates between biological processes in the body and mental consciousness. There is a method, called "biofeedback" and it is focused on controlling these processes.

Results of extensive scientific trials clearly show that every patient is able to learn how to control and modify some of the biological functions of his body, like the heartbeat, blood pressure or temperature, simply by using *visualization*. Thus, for those who wish to attain good health, it will be necessary to keep the harmony between four vital interconnected areas of their lives: physical, spiritual, psychological and societal.

Illness is a process, affected by many various factors – not just biological pathogens or genetic issues, but it is also profoundly determined by lifestyle, beliefs, attitude, and diet. Actually, there is one more, very important factor – the will of Life. This has a serious impact on the functioning of the immune and other innate disease fighting systems of the body. Impasse in life can lead to feelings of helplessness or hopelessness. This in turn may lead to the creation of pathological symptoms and finally manidfestation of serious illness.

Your happy morning

I would like to introduce one of the most useful mediation methods I have used.

When you first wake up, start the day with an honest smile. The new day is renewal and a good reason to be happy. Sit down on the floor and start with a few calm and slow stretching exercises.

When your body is warmed up, you will already start to feel the work of endorphins (these are the body's joy hormones). Now, close your eyes and meditate for a few minutes – you can sit or lie down. Your breath should become controlled, deliberate, and slow. Your mind will progressively become clear and free from all the negativity that encumbers it.

When you open your eyes, you should feel a refreshing peace and a strong precognition that everything will be as it should be today. You will feel safe, calm, and confident. You can easily think positively now.

Take a book with some motivational quotes, Bible, poetry, whatever you like, and read steadily and with understanding for 5 minutes. Then take a minute or two to reflect on the sense of what you have just read.

Try to make sure, that your schedule allows you to do 20 minutes of this ritual every morning. This simple routine will ensure that you are stronger each day and give you the power needed to face your everyday challenges.

The therapeutic power of friendship

Psychologist, Robert Ornstein, and Dr. David Sobel authored the book *Healthy Pleasures* where they detail their own vision of pleasure.

The human brain has many ways to transmit the signal of pleasure from one nerve cell to the other. What is interesting, is the evolution of our human ability to experience pleasure. Throughout the evolution process, all life has been given pleasures like eating or physical contact. Behaviours that lead to pleasure or success are self-reinforcing being more and more enjoyable.

Being rich, following a healthy diet and playing sports is not in and of itself enough to stay or become healthy and happy.

**The simplest and most direct path to happiness
is giving and caring about others.**

Nowadays, there are so many support and self-help groups, that everybody can participate in one. These groups supported by their own members help each other. Participation in these kind of meetings helps to fight the feeling of social isolation and loneliness, we all develop at some stage of life.

Teresa Seeman from the University of Southern California has described the societal ties of senior citizens. She interviewed almost 3 thousand people aged 65+, none of whom was living in a retirement or residential or nursing home. She came to the conclusion that for these people, it is important not only to have somebody close but also to have the ability to share with others important devlopments in their lives, and to share their emotions with friends or family. Having a wife or a husband doesn't always add up to the best emotional support. Children while a blessing, at some point can bring only material support, unfortunately not always the emotional assistance we need. When this happens, we may turn to our friends, colleaues, though it could be anyone who is truly able to listen empathize, support and understand. It doesn't even seem to matter if these people are physically close. What really matters is the will to help and being available when needed.

Support is more than just a physical presence.

Love and affection can be the deciding factor when it comes to crossing the thin line between health and sickness. All in all, this is exactly what decides when we're happy and empowered, or demotivated and sad.

Dr. Dean Ornish in his book *Love and survival* points out that the feeling of being supported and united with people surrounding you, has a crucial impact for your health. When you feel loved and surrounded by people who really care about you, you are happier and that equates to being simply healthier. The risk of becoming seriously ill at that point recedes, and even if illness happens, you have a much better chance for a quick recovery.

Love and loving relationships act like am emotional and physical shield. They profoundly influence the immune system and makes the body and mind more resistant. Dr. Pasteur once used a good metaphor to describe this situation. He said, that isolation and loneliness is a great environment for microbes and pathogens to grow. Pathogens both physical and mental. This is why all over the world, all successful cultures and nations cultivate unity and affection as a part of the tradition and spiritual life of their society.

Love is a phenomenon that is difficult to describe in words. Like a beautiful sunrise or sundet, we can all feel it, but sometimes struggle to fully describe it be it in words, music, or art. Everybody wants to experience it, which is why for ages, people have searched for some universal technique to find true love. It's important to say here, that intimacy shouldn't be only about love. It should be also about peace. Internal spiritual and emotional peace. Do you ever wonder what that is? It could be a feeling of full open-mindedness for everything that may or may not happen. It may also mean *trust* in the power of recovery. Or a complete readiness to live in harmony with everything happening in your life at this moment.

For me personally, this equates to an existence filled with love, affection, intimacy, true wisdom and spiritual bravery.

Music therapy

An often neglected aset on the long list of life's little pleasures is music. The strong connection between music and the process of physical and spiritual recovery was known to people even in ancient times. In the 19th century scientists became interested in the impact of music on the physical processes of the body, like the heartbeat, blood pressure or respiration. In 1986, the *Journal of Music Therapy* published the results of their analysis of 30 different pieces of research on the role of music in medical therapy and recovery from illness.

Music therapy is mostly used to help with the pain of fear and anxiety. Nowadays, there are some researches who have adopted music therapy as a technique to help with improving patients' physical and psychological condition. Calming, peaceful music can be used as a salve if not a cure for pain, fear depression, and despair. More stimulative and energetic kinds of music can be used to distract the patient from negative thoughts and emotions.

There is a common opinion that distraction techniques like relaxation, meditation, hypnosis or visualization are all very effective as a cure of pain. A lot of people have used this music therapy technique completely subconsciously. How many time have you self-medicated by listening to music thereby distracting yourself from negative emotions or mental suffering, or just to alleviate boredom?

Healthy laughter

It is almost universally held that natural happiness and laughter is good for us. And this is indeed true! A good laugh, joke or anything that make us smile has a soothing impact on the body and mind. It is one of those self-reinforcing pleasures discussed earlier in this chapter.

Dr. Hamillton House had conducted research on this phenomena. He has proven, that mortality rates of humans can be reduced by taking part in outdoor physical activities, however trivial including hiking trips, parties and sports events.

**So, let's laugh, let allow ourselves pleasurable
emotions and just simply enjoy the moment!**

Here are some activities that may help you stay in a good health:
Opera or theater or a concert
Enjoying the beauty of a nature
Walks on the beach
Going to an art gallery
– Enjoying painting or photography
Simple contact with other people : conversation for conversations' sake...

It's easy isn't it and so familiar to everyone?
Let us rediscover it again.

Let's love life all over again!!

Be attentive towards your body,
because it does not only belong to you.
If you are healthy,
it can also be useful
to your fellow men.

Chapter 2

The power of self-esteem

The way you think about yourself and others is pretty much affected by culture, upbringing, and personal history. The way you were raised may empower you or sometimes encumber you with some limits. That's why it's so important to know what most affects the way you see yourself and who you believe you actually are.

It is so common for us to judge others by the way they look, dress, or walk, in short by their appearance. Your opinion about somebody will be much better if their appearance matches your standards of excellence. A good example on how beauty standards and fashion are important for the society is, how many people struggle with eating disorders. This tragedy occurs all because people either eati to cover an unfilled emotional need, or because they want to make themselves into a body shape they feel others would admire. So many people today are trying to become perfect looking, while all the time ruining their bodies in the name of that idea. The appearance of perfection is not worth the sacrifice we pay for that type of transient self-esteem.

Self-esteem is extremely important for the way human beings function in any society. Those who are self-confident (not to be confused with pride), and possess a powerful will for life, often derive a higher satisfaction from their private and personal life. This is the basic nature of mental health and overall perception of well-being.

They way you think about yourself is a key to what and how you feel, and how you react to the world around you. One should constantly work on improving self-confidence in a constructive manner. Being fully conscious about your strengths and weaknesses is a clue. Don't expect yourself to be perfect! Nobody is. The most important thing here is to know that it's you yourself and your approach and attitudes that sculpt your life and interactions with the world around you. Remember, simply by the way you act, you can always affect people around you – the same way they affect you. This is a two-way relationship.

Most important in nurturing self-confidence is the first 4 years of a child's life. How easy to conclude then, that what really matters here is family life and the way parents bring up a young child. Adults have been responsible for creating your first thoughts about yourself, an effect that echoes thereafter throughout the rest of your life. That is why it is so important to accept a child the way he or she is, not the way you want him or her to be. We may guide in a urturing way, but we cannot dictate.

Remember, that you can't blame yourself for the things that you never had control over.

A simple analogy is between your self-esteem and your savings account. When you're doing something good for yourself and the others, you're building your confidence, and your savings are growing. When you're focused only on your career and material goods, letting anger and helplessness control your life – you're rapidly expending all of your savings of self-confidence.

What's important to you is your present life situation- not the past! Set aside all your failures of the past, the divorce, a death of somebody close, financial problems, depression all that really ruins your confidence and opinion about yourself. As long, as you're fail to understand that failures are natural for everybody and only temporary, you won't ever be able to advance. You must remember, and allow yourself the understanding that you are only human.

Nobody is perfect and you need to finally accept that. Everybody has a right to fall, as well as the right to expect the best, but not everyone has the courage and strength to grasp this reality. Always treat yourself for little successes and celebrate them. Little things really matter, because they spur you on to greater things.

Treat your body like a temple – remember about the little pleasures, at least once a week, something bigger once every two weeks, and something really special ones from time to time.

How have you ever thought about what you achieved in your life? Think, about what would you say to your friend after any achievement and keep repeating it to yourself. Congratulate yourself. Isn't it so easy to treat yourself with a nice long walk or a massage. Maybe you like a sweet treat like a piece of cake, or a pretty flower? Do it for yourself, why not?

Praising yourself is both easy and effective. If you use it right, it can really make a difference. When you accept yourself and your body – it's easier to appreciate what you really want and achieve it. A healthy body can perfectly recognize its own needs and, what's important here, also the moments when it needs more attention or help.

Everybody talks all the time about how to stay in shape and work on that beautiful body. You can easily get so much advice on how to achieve a perfect shape or weight or that perfect skin. On the other hand, have you ever heard any good advice how to care about your mind or spiritual well-being? How to respect your body? You're listening to the noise of everybody around you, but not listening to that quiet internal voice – to yourself and your needs.

You should always remember that your body is like your best friend, and you should accept it the way it is. It may not be perfect, but it is what it is, and it can sustain your healthy life.

Thinking positively is about expressing yourself as somebody who is happy – make people around you see you as someone who is uplifting and fulfilled, ready to give to others what they have discovered for themselves. That is a wonderful form of good-will.

Instead of "no more" say "let's try again".

Instead of "I won't ever get better" say "I will care about myself and I will be OK, I must TRY".

Thinking positive makes your mind expect the success and somehow pushes your actions into a path where you can really accomplish your goals. Don't ever complain (sometimes it seems the only thing to relieve frustration)– unfortunately the act of complaining makes your mind close in on itself only with negative thoughts, and then progress will be impossible. Every word you utter has energy – why would you want to surround yourself with negative energy? Bad or negative thoughts bring bout only bad outcomes – everybody knows that. When you're thinking positive, your life can only become better!

Positive thinking is also insightful to you, because it helps to realize what to actually do to improve your life. You should look at yourself realistically, and see yourself the way you are, not a fantasy, or the way you think somebody would want to see you. Don't fulfill somebody elses expectations, fulfil your own! This is the best way to improve your self-confidence – and the only proven way to lasting happiness.

If we learn to give ourselves to life confidently
and look with the eyes of the child
at what happens to us,
we can face the world
without damage to our soul.

Chapter 3

Positive thinking

Positive thinking is crucial not only for your mental, but also physical health. In ancient times, in the 5th-century B.C.E, the greek physician Hippocrates (one of the fathers of modern medicine) taught about the incredible power of people's natural ability for self-help. It seems he knew what we know also is true: that if you really want something to happen, it can and will happen sooner or later.

First of all, learn how to think positively about yourself. I'm sure you don't like it when somebody calls you names. Why are you doing it to yourself by thinking about yourself as a "failure", a "looser" somebody "not good enough"? Criticizing yourself won't bring about anything good, trust me. I bet, you have never thought so many terrible things about any of your friends or acquintances as you have about yourself. Why be so hard on yourself?

You cannot change what happened in the past. Better to focus on healing, rebuilding your self-esteem, and improving your strengths. Start using some relaxation techniques, doing some sports, dancing, or volunteering to help other people. This will create a great foundation for improvement. Giving is a good way to stop concentrating on all the past and all the negativity.

Listen to yourself. Treat your body, mind, and spirit as a whole, not three different things. When one part is suffering, the others are too. When your body is sick, your mind is not well too. You can't make it better by complaining about your state and blaming yourself for what is happening or has happened. If you are truly at fault, forgive yourself and change for the future. Remember, you can't change the past anyways.

Look at the mirror of reality and accept yourself. Remember the singularity of existence, that you are one and only in the whole world there is only one you. You must be a miracle because life is a miracle. Your body is the shield, that protects you from all the potential danger of the outside world. Treat it well. Beauty is illusory, at best temporary and inevitably self destructs. But that goodness that resides inside you – your "internal beauty" will stay with you beyond the present past and forever.

Prepare a list of all the successes in your life – the spectacular ones and even the ones that brought you only a few steps forward. Believe me, that list will be long. Remind yourself how happy and proud you were, remember the emotions, enthusiasm, the feeling of being empowered to do anything. Visualize it. Keep this feeling in your heart always and use it when you're feeling down or blue. Bring these moments back anytime you want and feeling them again when you need it. Use these emotions to be happy. Right here, right now. Make thinking about all these good moments a little ritual in your everyday life that helps you to stay in control of everything you are doing.

Appreciate every single experience that life affords you. Everything you went through was and is priceless, an incredible lesson for the remainder of your life.

To think positively you need endorphins – the "hormones of happiness". Endorphin levels in your body rise as you exercise. Instead of using medications or stimulant drugs to make yourself feel better, go outside and move, run, walk, go to the movies, meet with your friends. Do whatever you like and whatever makes you feel good. It is that easy!

Make natural endorphins your biologic addiction - it will make you feel happier, calmer, help control destructive emotions and help work problems out rationally. These little (but how important) chemical substances in your body function as a tool to measure your happiness. Scientists have been able to test how this process works in the human body. Results of this research has been crucial for progress in the fields of neurology and psychology.

In the first chapter, we discussed what biofeedback is. That was another important discovery of 20th-century physiology – thanks to this discovery, doctors now know, how the human brain can simultaneously control so many complex biochemical processes in the body. Use that knowledge! Do you know, that you can cure a headache sometimes by using only your will power? In so many cases of illness, even really serious disease, positive thinking can make a difference in hastening the recovery!

At every second your body is producing 6 million new blood cells, and at the same time another 6 million are dying. Your body has the never ending ability to renew. You're probably asking yourself now, if you can use that to keep your youth longer? Yes, you can! With a good diet and the right self-care program, science has shown that one can delay the aging processes by about 12-20 years, possibly even 30-40 years.

Does it mean that the key to aging is in your mind and attitude? Yes, I believe it does! Laziness and negligence in exercising, bad eating habits, failibg to utilize relaxation and breathing techniques, lack of passion in life and some moving interest – here are some of the things that are accelerate aging. Remember, you are in control, and it is only you who have the power to change your own situation!

Always stay positive.
Don't let the negative thoughts take over your mind.
Keep the negativity away with the shield of a positive attitude and the will to stay young and active.

Aging is all about losing the balance between old and new cells in your body. Your brain does have the power to slow it and control it. By using only 10% of the brain's abilities you can delay this aging processes.

Here's one recipe for an elixir of long life – positive thoughts, emotions, and feelings. Simple, isn't it? Love is the best medication for every illness. Amor vincit omnia.

By loving and accepting yourself you can fix your attitude and bad habits. When you like yourself, you like the world around you. This helps maintain harmony and this harmony is one key to a better life. All that is really easy and effective, is connected together.

Your mind has no limits.

Everybody wants to be happy. Everybody has a right to it. On your way to it, you are obviously going to face some obstacles, but you should never let them stop you. The power of your mind is in actuality unlimited and you can face it and fight back.

What can slow you down on your way to happiness?
- wrong eating habits,
- infections,
- shortage of sunlight,
- bad air quality,
- tiredness,
- overworking and stress,
- anxiety,
- no physical exercise,
- lack of good sleep,
- wrong breathing techniques,
- negative feeling and emotions,
- pessimism.

Dr. Marian Pomorski emphasizes the important role of a patient's attitude. Every thought has its own power, and all these thoughts together create your life – for better or worse. You're the one in power here.

**Always remember, that positive thinking
invariably leads to positive actions.**

So, change your way of thinking. Believe yourself every day, that you can be happy and having everything you need. The key to achieving your goals is in the way you think about your abilities to accomplish it. Stay positive and make it happen.

You are the exact same person you created in your thoughts.

Everybody, who lacks self-esteem is "sentenced" to be average. To become successful you have to self-believe, that you are good enough to achieve every goal. Trying believing that you are important, then feel like it. You know something? Once you succeed in feeling like this, you become more powerful in achieving your goals.

By staying in harmony with your conscience you will free yourself from guilt. Blaming yourself for everything is an extremely destructive feeling. Practice yourself blocking these destructive thoughts and you will automatically become more successful.

Forget about the failures, stop thinking about it. If your thoughts are going into the past – focus on positive memories, don't let the bad ones come back to you. You don't need them. Getting rid of them is a big step in fighting with fears, anxieties, and depression.

Let's think about what is really making you happy. Realize, that it's not just fate but your decisions, plans, and actions. Your own positive attitude is what's making you happy. If you're a successful person, failure won't destroy you. It will be just another constructive lesson that you will use in future to become stronger and avoid the same mistakes again.

Don't waste your time on thinking "what if".
By following these rules, you will see changes in your life. Don't count on good luck. Count on yourself. Focus on developing the strengths and character that will lead you to success.

Make your age a strength, not a weakness. You are never too old to follow your dreams!

While you are making your plans for the future, focus on the things that give you pleasure. Something really important and meaningful for you. Otherwise, you can do whatever you want. Happiness has no age limits. Remember, the best is yet to come!

Stop complaining about your health and use your energy to enjoy your time. Appreciate your life and health. These changes will help you fight any illnesses you're struggling with. Always remember sometimes it is matter of perspective, your life is often better than you think it is. You just need to start enjoying and appreciating it.

Be happy with what you have.

Life is to enjoy! Don't waste it on complaining.

I will remove from my vocabulary such words as
„I would be",
„I would have"
„I should",
„I would have to",
„I would do."
They indicate
that I do not live in the present,
but in the world of illusion,
without seeing
what is real.

Chapter 4

Forgiving

Forgiving is a big challenge. It's not easy, especially, when you're feeling angry. However, it really helps to move on and stay free from negative emotions and thoughts. Don't let the anger to impact your mind and, in effect, destroy your harmony and health. This leads you only into harming yourself, not the person or situation you are blaming for your unhappiness.

The most important idea is to stay open and free from anger and hate. It doesn't matter if you forgive somebody or yourself – it always brings relief. Also, don't ever hesitate to ask for forgiveness either from others or yourself.

You have to learn how to forgive yourself. It's as hard perhaps harder than forgiving another person.

The love that you're giving yourself and others is an enormous and endless power that you can use to help yourself forget about the past, about people hurting you and the hurting you may have caused others.

Never forget that you are in charge of your feelings and emotions, and you control them. Use this knowledge and find peace within yourself. Learn how to forgive.

Your internal beauty

Have you ever watched somebody who is really happy? Being joyful, energetic, motivated and self-confident? Did you ever feel that this person is good looking? What was really attractive to you was the charisma, not the "physical" beauty. This is what we can call "internal beauty". Real beauty is internal. This is the gold standard in beauty that attracts people the most.

If you're living in total harmony, you know what is important for your mind. You know, what makes you feel calm. Which means that you already know, how to make yourself healthy and beautiful.

A calm and happy person is more attractive to others, also in intimate situations. Being self-confident and accepting yourself is what makes you look pretty in the eyes of your partner. Make your internal beauty glow and grow. Take time for yourself, think about your needs. Meditation and exercises are often helpful here. It will really make you look younger, more energetic, and full of vitality.

There are many ways to work on your internal beauty. Quiet time reserved only for you, humming a favorite song, silent prayer. Doing something that you simply enjoy doing will help you stay in harmony with your psyche. Remember, to stay consistent and make it an everyday ritual. Try to practice keeping harmony between body and mind, no matter what is happening in your life. this is a good way to reach peace and happiness.

SWB   KRASNOWSKI   3.03.2004

You say
that you are happy in a relationship.
So why don't you more often thank the other person
for sharing the joy and the pain with you
and that they chose you among so many other people?

SMB   KRASNOLUDEK   3.03.2009

Chapter 5

Age and stay classy

Aging and keeping your charm and glamour is possible only if you care about your health. A good balanced diet, lots of water, regular exercise and relaxation – all of these will help you stay in good shape.

The message here is simple: **If you are healthy and feeling good, you are beautiful.**

Another important thing at this point is a good mood – it goes together with harmony between body and mind. You need to find your peace in life. Even, if you are a very active person, you have to think about some quiet time alone, just for yourself. Meditation, relaxation, prayer, yoga, listening to the music, reading – whatever you choose, it must be a good way to care about your psyche.

Keep your energy, open-mindedness and zest for life!

When you age, many processes in your metabolism are slowing down – your body has to obviously change. Don't worry, accept it! It's a natural process. Every stage of life has its own rights and rules, don't try to fight them. Enjoy these changes, you look beautiful, you are beautiful!

Some people say: "you are as old as you feel". This saying cannot be closer to the truth. Your mood and health are in your hands, so think young, and stay young!

Everybody wants to be happy and find an ultimate way to that state. The question is – how to do it? I have a few useful tips for you!

Be honest in self-criticism. When you are able to realize and understand your mistakes and weaknesses, you will be able to fight and correct them! This is the best path to perfection.

Analyze your failures. Don't just blame bad luck – everyone meets misfortune by chance, how we respond is the important thing. It's you, whois in charge. Find out what cause the problem and then work this thing out.

Learn from your mistakes – analyze, find good reasons and constructive solutions, then take the path to success.

Always stay focused on your goals – never forget or give up. Stay strong and enjoy the efforts you are making to sculpt your life the way you want it to be.

Remember, that every situation in your life has some good side to it, even if it is hard to see it at that moment. Try to always find the best in a situation and keep believing in yourself.

Start every day with a smile and enjoy each small new beginning. Feel the joy and keep going upwards through your life. Following your dreams and goals will make you happy.

Try to find energy and inspiration in everything you do. Work on a positive attitude that will then work for you.

Remember, there is always a solution!

Change all your bad habits. If the reality that you were growing into is holding you down – fight it! You have no control on past events now, don't blame yourself for them and don't treat the past as a reason to give up. No matter how difficult your life used to be, you can still be happy in the future.

The essential thing to do is to consider your whole life as a living breathing organism, producing new cells to renew itself, sometimes getting sick, and expelling everything that is unnecessary and un-healthy.

Can you imagine your body getting rid of unhealthy by products of life only once every 5 years? No? Why would you then do that to your mind? Your path to happiness needs CONSTANT effort. Once learned things won't stay with you forever, you need to practice. That's why you need to care about yourself every day, not from time to time, only when you need it. Your success needs tender loving care.

Life, like every living organism there are good times and bad times, this is only natural, it must be accepted. You need to care about your mental and spiritual growth, your physical exercise and rest - this will keep your energy on a high level. You will be calmer and at the same time, stronger. You just need to remember to never stop working on it, and always be proactive.

To keep your joy, you need to care about it. Sometimes, you will need to fight to make yourself stronger.

How to make your mind impact your body?

You already know, that the power of the mind can be really effective in treating many diseases, pain, insomnia, and even cancer.

Positive thinking is a thing you can learn for yourself. An important idea is to make it a habit, part of your everyday routine. You need to get rid of all the negative emotions. Do something good for somebody, help your friend, a neighbor, volunteer for your community. Being open, is not only for yourself but also for other people. This will instantly make you feel better.

Focus more on your successes than failures. That will help you find peace and satisfaction. Practice praising yourself for everything you did right, while not overly dwelling on your mistakes. Keep a positive internal dialogue. Be happy with all the good things that happened to you and don't spend too much time analyzing the bad moments. Every day find some time for contemplation especially all the positive things in your life. Close your eyes, meditate – imagine the sunlight, a scenic view, bring a beautiful memory from your childhood.

Start writing a journal. Every day put in it some positive thoughts and things you feel you are grateful for. You will very quickly realize, how many things you have worth having. Going back to re-read all of this later will help you building your positive attitude and improve your self-esteem.

**If you begin to think, that you are feeling good,
you will actually start feeling better.**

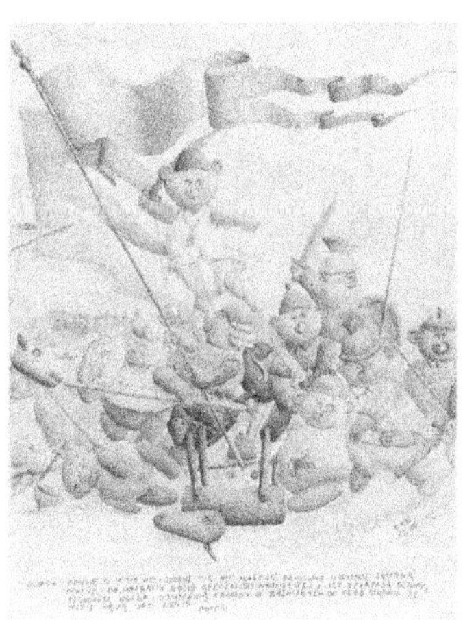

If you focus on your breath,
you will find
that you are becoming calmer.

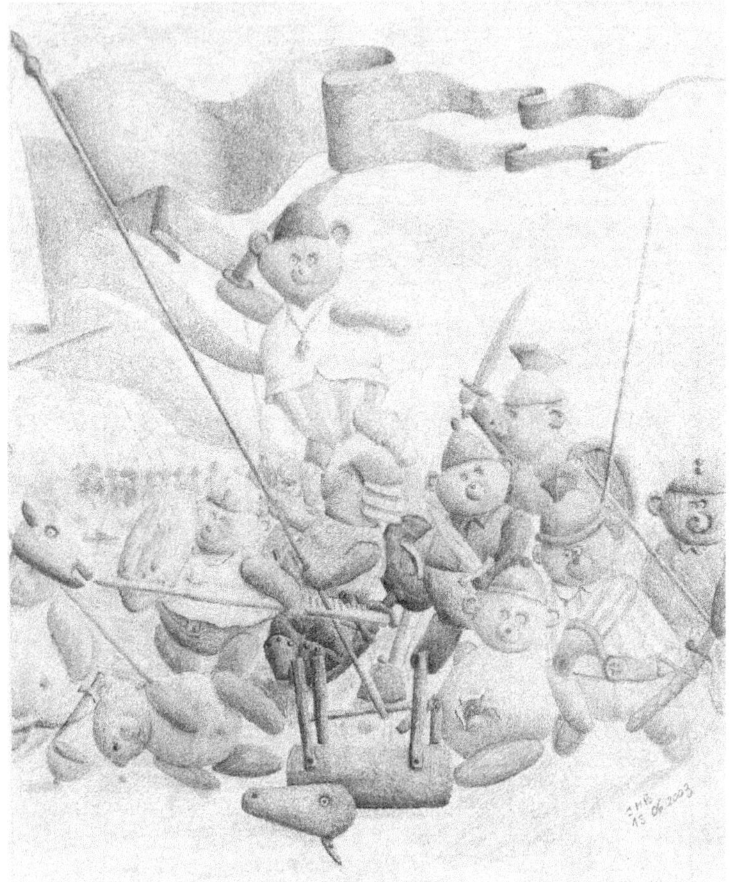

UWAGA PROSZĘ O MISIE USZKODZONE SIĘ NIE MARTWIĆ PONIEWAŻ WSZYSTKIE ZOSTANĄ
ODDANE DO NAPRAWY GDZIE SPECJALIŚCI NAJWYŻSZEJ KLASY ZAŁATAJĄ DZIURY,
PRZYSZYJĄ OCZKA I UZUPEŁNIĄ TROCINY W BRZUSZKACH DO TEGO STOPNIA, ŻE
MISIE BĘDĄ JAK NOWE AUTOR

Chapter 6

Healing power of emotions

Emotions have more impact on your life than you might suppose. We do not realize this emotional power until it causes depression or some other serious problem. Everybody knows that extreme stress can easily lead to a heart attack- we hear about it after natural disasters such as earthquakes or floods. But there is a myriad of bad effects that arise from negative stress. On the other hand, we can harness the beneficial effects of positive emotions.

Emotions can heal you and make you happy. Let's learn how to make them your biggest strength!

The power of the psyche actually depends on the full usage of the potential of your thoughts and emotions. By using it you can recover or enhance your mental and physical harmony. You can use it in so many ways to make your life better, easier and more productive. There are some exercises that can help you achieve this and use your full potential. However, it requires a lot of discipline and patience. This kind of training and exercises may be used to help you fall asleep, calm down in a stressful situation, find your peace before an important meeting or event, and fight with fear depression or anger.

There is a very strong connection between emotions and attitude, and this in turn leads to control of many important functions of your body. All the systems in your body are connected together, and completely depend on each other. You can help them work not only by simple positive thinking, but also by using some mental training techniques. Every system may be more or less affected by those techniques - so it's worth a try. It will make you feel fulfilled and satisfied.

All the symptoms of most diseases are alarm signals for you. You need to learn how to read these signals and understand them. Your body is trying to send you a message: "change something, please help me - then you will feel better". It's better to not to ignore these messages.

You should realize, that a doctor would can only help you to recover. Most of the job is on you, and your mind. You have to focus on the healing process – this is how self-help works. Doctors and medical treatments do not remove the ultimate responsibility from you. To get better you have to want it and help your body achieve it!

Of course, there are negative and positive emotions. Your role here is to control them and learn how to use them for your own good. The power of your mind is crucial here. In the past, emotions were mostly the object of philosophy and psychology, not science. What is more, at the beginning of human evolution, emotions were only used as a way to communicate – so emotions are older and even more natural than languages.

Darwin was the first scientist, who analyzed and tested emotions. It was a basis for his further researches and discoveries. In 1882 he had finally proved that some of the emotions are universal, and you can meet them in all cultures. Basic emotions like fear, joy, aversion, anger, sadness and so on, are determined genetically.

Unfortunately, in the modern world, the role of emotions is becoming less and less important. It is astonishing how we have let this happen and lost control in such a basic area of our life. This tendency is causing many of the modern diseases that people are struggling with.

Our ancestors knew how to exhibit their emotions and use them in communication - a perfect tool in communication with people around us but also, with yourself. Anyway, even more important than the ability to display emotions is an understanding of their impact on your body and psyche. Many of the processes in your body are dependent on our emotions. Yes, this means that your life may depend on them.

Treat others with love

If you want to find the key to affection and real connection with others, you first have to find respect and love for yourself.

If you maintain a good relationship with yourself, you can experience closer affection with people important to you. You need to learn to understand every emotion you experience. This is the only way to find inner peace, sympathy, and understanding. If you're not able to connect with yourself, how could you ever connect with others.

Your emotions do matter.

Don't forget about meditation and relaxation

The most important aspect of meditation is the ability to relax, to calm down completely and focus. It's not easy, especially in the modern world, when we are pre-occupied all the time with career, money, family, or friends. Technology has intruded rather than liberated our lives also. All of this has a serious impact on our mind.

There are hundreds of different techniques of meditation. Most of us, when it comes to meditation think that this is about sitting on the floor with your legs crossed and staring intothe distance. It doesn't really have to look like this. You can meditate wherever you want, whenever you want, if only you are able to concentrate. You can sit on a chair, go for a walk or lie down in your bed. It is as though your concentration brings you to the point, where everything around ceases to exist for you at that moment. But, you are fully conscious of what you are doing. The truth is, most of us have experienced this many times and didn't even realize, that this was in actuality meditation.

What is common to every kind of meditation is the mental focusing on something even nothing. It could be facilitated by slow walking or controlled breathing. You just need to put *all* your mind and attention on this, nothing else can distract you. For example, in walking, you concentrate on every step, every movement - the moment when your foot is touching or leaving the ground and the beginning of every new step.

When you are focused enough, no other thoughts will distract you or intrude on your mind. All the surroundings will disappear. Your body will be fully relaxed and loose. You begin to feel free from tension, anger, fatigue, in short your body will be visibly slowing down. This is how meditation works, even if you do not realize that any of these processes are happening. This is now meditation has such an incredible impact on our body and health. When you feel too much tension or anger and it is hard to "turn off" all the emotions, control is only possible to learn with careful and regular meditation.

While meditating, you're focusing on something very basic and easy. You are concentrating on your breath slowing down deliberately more and more. Your mind is also calming down and relaxing. This is an easy way to feel better and you can make it into a daily habit, to improve your life. These habits will also help you manage your time, especially if you are a busy person and always lacking time for yourself. One small thing with so many advantages. From less tension and stress, to better time management. The more concentrated you are on practicing this method, the more advantages you can experience.

Remember, that relaxation and time for rest is the key to a healthy life. It helps us face stress and bring back homeostasis and energy to your life. Always take a few minutes to relax both before and after every meditation session. This is important for your ability to concentrate. You can use activities that help make you more relaxed: a hot bath, relaxing music, yoga - whatever you fancy.

Attentive walking

This is a powerful meditation technique you may like and is very useful as an exercise to practise concentration and self-consciousness. It is also very simple, enjoyable, and easy. You can do it while taking your stroll around the neighborhood or even when you are going to work. Focus on your breathing, don't think about the past or the future. Be there, at the moment. Remember to keep your back straight while walking. The ancients believed that the primal force of life is transmitted up and down the spine.

Put all your attention into walking, be fully aware of every step you take. Focus on the movement of your feet, arms, and shoulders. Feel the fresh air on your face.

The next step is being aware of your surroundings. Where are you? Who is there with you? Listen to the sounds around you, smell all the scents, notice every color. Try not to just notice as much as *be aware* as much as you can. Focus on your feelings, emotions, and your reactions to every stimulus.

Stay meditative

People, who are meditative are far more open to the signals from their body. They are able to understand themselves better. This kind of consciousness is a key to mental health and positive mood. It is also exciting and can bring about a feeling of complete freedom.

The world needs you exactly the way you are. You don't need to try to be somebody else. Be yourself, love yourself, be happy with life. Above all love yourself!

Try to understand your partner. In good relationships, partners are like each other's reflections – it's entirely based on understanding and full acceptance.

You need to understand that if your partner acts exactly the way you want them to act, he or she would not truly be himself any more. This wouldn't be the person you fell in love with.

Happiness is something that you have to build inside of yourself. Remember, that your partner can help you with that. You can be happy together, no matter what happens.

Try to be more aware of your partner's needs. Ask directly - "How can I make you happy?". This is the surest way to happiness for both of you.

Just one day
spent in absolute peace
is equal to one day
of immortality.

Chapter 7

Revitalization

Even the oldest medical tests, done in ancient Mesopotamia, proved that human health is strongly connected with the natural harmony of the seasons and other living cycles. You cannot detach yourself from nature, that would mean a life lacking in natural harmony and, as such an effect called sickness.

Your eating habits are extremely important for your life quality and the pace of aging. The way you have eaten in the past can clearly affect your health as you mature in age. This is why a balanced diet is so important in revitalization as we mature.

The diet you adopt should be a fully conscious process. It is, all in all, a crucial factor in the way to radical changes in your body, in orer to become healthier and bring back your natural power and vigor.

Heiser said that if somebody is able to maintain a healthy diet it would make that person capable of achieving anything.

Eating has 3 basic functions:
1. nutritional,
2. as a pleasure stimulant,
3. as a social event.

When we have more food than is necessary for our survival, eating is becomes a pleasure, not just a nutritional necessity.

Eating is commonly perceived as a positive stimulant to the senses and body. Food should be tasty and attractive in order to make you want to eat it. At some point, there is an important question everyone should ask themselves. Why am I making myself eat this even if my body is not showing any symptoms of hunger?
When you are really hungry, there is no need for food to be especially good. Everything would taste amazing. On the other hand, when you are hungry but not feeling like eating, that means that your body is struggling with some illness or toxins. Low appetite is an obvious sign of a problem.

Is it possible to be a foodie and follow a good diet? Not really. In that case, you probably carve fancy, attractive and gourmet meals. This is in opposition to what your body really needs – simple and natural food. Gourmet food also needs a lot of cooking and processing. That kills all the best nutritional elements and making it less valuable for your body.

Very important to your appetite are all the substances that are stimulating to your nervous system. By smelling and looking at food your brain is firing up your appetite for this food. This makes your brain react very similar to what happens when one craves caffeine and sees it. One desires it.

Bircher-Benner, the famous Swiss dietitian often compared the feeling after eating meat to the sated mood of a heavy drinker after drinking. This is why women should avoid meat at times of increased activity of the nervous system – for example the pre-menstrual period (PMS) or menopause.

Did you know, that vegetarians have a better muscle efficiency when it comes to physical activities? Meat is toxic and in many ways, it poisons your body.

In the 19th century Bircher-Benner founded a nursing home where the main therapy was a vegetarian diet. He was proving, that solar energy, produced and kept by plants using the photosynthesis process is also a good nutrient for humans. He was strongly recommending eating only plant-based products as the best source of energy.
He also said, that to keep the full harmony of the body people should base their diet on at least 50% of raw edible products.

Over 100 years ago, Iljicz Miecznikov emphasized the same fact, that one of the main factors in aging is intestinal diseases caused by the after-effects of eating meat. He was proving, that a meat-based diet causes the increased presence of toxins to a dangerous level where the body cannot get rid of them by its natural processes.

A good natural-revitalization diet for mature people should follow two essential rules:
No overloading. Moderation is the rule.
In every sense of the word – it's not only about calories or your body weight. Every substance in excess can cause many serious problems.
Diversification.
You need to remember to supply your body with all the necessary nutrients, but there must be high quality and biological value to your meals. The more processed the food is, the less value it has for your body.

It's extremely important to also remember, that a diet should be personalized. Everybody has different needs. People with specific nutritional deficits, those who are overweight or malnourished, or those who are very physically active –all have differing requirements in a diet.

Benefits of fatty acids

Almost every day now one hears about a new study proving the beneficial influence of polyunsaturated fatty acids on the human body. The most valuable of all, Omega-3 fatty acids, can influence many bodily functions:
regulation of blood coagulability,
preventing of atherosclerosis,
maintain musculoskeletal function including the condition of our muscles and tendons.

Omega-3 fatty acids are also important for fighting the diseases of heart, skin, and joints. What is more, they may have great benefit to the treatment processes of many serious illnesses such as, Alzheimer disease. Do you want more encouraging news? Omega-3 fatty acids help with the absorption of calcium that directly improves the condition of skin, hair, and nails. Last, but not least, Omega-3's boost the function of your immune system. We are just beginning realizethe full benefits of omega 3 fatty acids.

Doesn't it seem like Omega-3 fatty acids can make your life better and healthier? That's why it's important to remember about providing it in your diet!

The best natural source of Omega-3 acids is fish and seafood. Eating these at least 3 times a week is one secret to a healthy long life. You can also provide it by eating tofu, almonds, walnuts and some kind of oils – canola or linseed. However, eating fish is the easiest (and the best) way to supply your body with this incredibly valuable nutrient with so many benefits.

If I want to learn
to accept other people unconditionally,
first I have to learn
to accept myself.

Chapter 8

The Revitalization Diet

How aging works and how to prevent it.

Aging of an organism is causing loss of internal balance and harmony and thus significant increases the risk of infections and diseases. Aging impairs the basic functions of cells, organs and whole systems. It also weakens the immune system and impairs your ability to fight potential disease causing pathogens.

Environmental and dietetic factors may be crucial here. By avoiding or minimizing the impact of harmful substances and habits you can directly and positively boost your longevity. The definition of good health is simple – your state of being is completely dependent on the condition of your internal organs. Peak physical and mental condition needs not only the absence of disease, but also possibly the highest functionality of every organ. That requires training. You should keep in mind the role of regular physical activity, simple, hygienic lifestyle, and a balanced, personalized diet. The salutary benefits are noticeable in the function of all organs. It will also significantly enhance your immunity.

The main methods of prevention, treatment, and revitalization are:
- *kinesiotherapy* – therapeutic treatment of exercise and massage,
- *dietetic therapy* – the therapeutic use of diet,
- *ergotherapy* – use of physical effort and activities in the treatment,
- *psychotherapy*, aims to improve an individual's well-being and mental health, to resolve or mitigate troublesome behaviors, beliefs, compulsions, thoughts, or emotions, and to improve relationships and social skills.
- *pharmacotherapy* – the therapeutic use of medical drugs.

Exercising = health = life

It's nothing innovative - everybody knows, that any physical activity is good for their body and mind. However, many people still don't follow that simple advice. I have just given you some basic and simple rules to follow to keep your energy, health, and longevity. This is also the source of essential power for your body to function.

Physical activity is crucial for optimal body function. As we age, it also has the power of revitalization. Body cells and neurons should be constantly stimulated. Lack of stimulation causes degeneration or even cell death. Physical activity, on the other hand, causes dilation of arteries which leads to better blood supply to the whole body. All bodily organs become stronger and more active, especially the heart and circulation. Everyday simple exercises are crucial and extremely important for the optimal functioning of your heart! Even walking daily has been shown to improve longevity.

Power of nature

Your body is like our Planet Earth – it is very sensitive to the depletion of its natural sources and whatever artificially changes its normal functioning. People who are living in harmony with nature are less easily to experience such harmful changes. What matters the most is not how you look, but how you feel.

There is no one "recipe" for a perfect, harmonious, beautiful body. The age and shape of the body shouldn't really matter. What's important is how your body feels. Are you really looking for yourself? Are you able to read and react to all the "messages" from your body? Only this way will you be able to fully enjoy the full spectrum of feelings and emotions.

Nature wants you to experience pleasure, to be able to communicate with your heart and spirit, and sometimes maybe experience a little bit of craziness? It's all natural. Do you have the ability to feel joy and happiness? Do you sometimes swing and dance to the rhythm of the music? When you do, nothing else matters.

Instead of focusing on your appearance, spend more time thinking about what's deeper – about your soulyou're your internal, natural beauty. Insecurities and fear about acceptance are taking your creativity away, demotivating you and making you feeling unfulfilled. That's not what you need, is it?

Effects of aging treatment

There are many treatment methods and medications used in the revitalization of the body and to slow down the aging process. Here are the effects of some of these treatments:
1. Preventing or even reducing the effects of atherosclerosis, dilation of arteries, improving the blood circulation.
2. Boosting the clearance of harmful substances like waste products from cells.
3. Destroying and removing old atrophied cells and simultaneously "mobilizing" the body to regenerate and producing new, fully functional cells.
4. Stimulation of the nervous system and improving neural functioning..
5. Counteracting on the damaging actions of harmful circulating free radicals.
6. Supplying the body with all the essentialsubstances that it's lacking – hormones, vitamins, nucleic acids.
7. Reducing the effects of aging on DNA.

Autotherapy techniques

Autotherapy begins in your head. This is the incredible power of our own mind and consciousness. You should learn how to relax your body and focus on your whole psyche each session of treatment.
You must imagine and visualize your health problem and then focus all your mind on fixing it. Feel some sympathy and love for that struggling part of your body. You have to be really firm with all your thoughts. Put one hand on the spot you consider to be sick and transfer the positive energy from the outside of your body, from your environment. This is how you neutralize what is bad inside by bringing something good from outside. Stay calm, relaxed and focused. By relaxing your mind you are also allowing your nervous system to calm down and relax. The best medications you need are faith, that you have the power to fight the illness, hope in full recovery and self-love. This is a dose of positive energy that will empower your body and mind, and undoubtedly lead you on your way back to good health.

Self-treatment uses the essential energy from three sources, which are the vital elements: air, earth, and sun. Every person is able to absorb and use this kind of natural energy. It becomes a completely unconscious process. The energy you derive is from the air you breathe, from the earth by walking, and from the sun by just simple contact with sunlight. Thanks to this you can keep your body and mind in natural harmony. By fulfilling your aura with this vital energy you're supplying it to every single cell of your body. While purifying your soul you are also curing your body.

**To find your health and happiness you
first need to find your harmony**

What is harmful for your body?

Civilization is bringing us many harmful factors. You face them every day. What are they?

- Bad diet and eating habits.

- Lack of physical activity.

- Poor clothing.

- Overstimulation of the senses.

- Pollution.

- Addictions.

- Stress and overwork.

Hormone of youth

The hormone of youth – dehydroepiandrosterone or androsterones (DHEA) is produced by the adrenal glands. When your body is not producing enough of this substance, there is thinning of the skin, weakening of muscles and connective tissues become frailer. Also, one's overall constitution changes – it becomes harder to deal with the stress and strain of everyday challenges. The will for life becomes less and less powerful as does many other body functions. DHEA is crucial for your body.

Studies show that we are able to control on some level the production of this hormone. Its presence and concentration a depend a lot on the level of our physical activity. This is why some people start to age more rapidly right after the beginning of retirement. If you don't have a good plan for your life after retirement, this is what's going to happen.

Outdoor exercises a good opportunity to supply your body with oxygen and stimulate your body's metabolism. An active person equates to a happy person. Long life doesn't mean staying old for the longest time possible. It means keeping your youth for as long as possible. If you could ask some of the 100 years old people about their past, you can be sure you would never hear anything about slowing down after their 50th birthday.

To summarize: Stay active to keep your youth.

Kinesiotherapy

This method is based on curing and preventing illness by physical exercise and massage. Using *kinesiotherapy* can bring back the physical abilities you thought lost many years ago. It makes coming back to activity easier, and stops wrong habits developing in your movement. It also protects against premature degeneration of the skeleton and muscular system. Thus, one can prevent many complications of the circulatory and respiratory systems. All these benefits are derived only by being active.

Kinesiotherapy is not only used in recovery from many muscular injuries, dysfunction or pain but also after cerebrovascular accidents (strokes), heart attacks, some respiratory system diseases such as cystic fibrosis, rheumatic problems, and in recovery after many surgeries. Sometimes, it may be used as a stand alone treatment and sometimes as an addition to other methods. When necessary, kinesiotherapy can be used both before and after surgery. In any case, it is important to remember continue other methods in conjunction with kinesiotherapy, if they are recommended.

Physical exercises

Regular exercise can help you with digestion and metabolism, removing unwanted toxins and waste products from your body and of course keeping your muscles in good shape. There are profound advantages of exercise appropriate to age and conditioning for everybody, that's a fact. The most important thing here is to stay systematic and exercise regularly. A good method in selecting the right intensity for you is using half of your capability. If you routinely tire after 40 minutes of running, then a perfect length of training for you would be 20 minutes. Frequently, when people lose their motivation after the first few days of physical activity, they just give up. To avoid that situation, invite someone motivated to exercise with you - your partner, friend, or neighbor. Isn't it easier to make sport a part of your daily routine when you're not all alone with the challenge, especially the first time. Remember to exercise a little bit every day, even if it is only for a few minutes. For example, a short walk after a meal can help you with the digestive process. A regular walk is a good method to prevent heart attacks or a stroke. The chances of such diseases are more than 40% reduced for active people. Physicians universally endorse exercise as a way to reduce cholesterol levels, blood pressure, body weight, and blood sugar.

Exercising is the key to long life and good health.

Breathing techniques are important for mind and body control

Efficient utilization of oxygen is an essential part of respiration.

By using the proper techniques, you can slow down the aging process. In most published studies, active people have been shown to live as much as 30-40 years longer than sedentary individuals. China sets a good example for all of us in this regard. Many Chinese regularly spend some time every day on breathing and performing a graceful series of continuous flowing movement exercises that improve balance, strengthen the body, and reduce stress. It is said that such exercise can improve longevity and well-being. Certainly, the rate of elderly people with cancer is way lower than in Europe and North America. When any organism gets older, more and more cells suffer a decline in oxidative respiration which means getting less oxygen. This leads to many diseases including diabetes, hypertension, as well as circulatory and digestive system problems.
By breathing, the entire body is supplied with natural vital energy produced within each cell, that keeps all living processes going. As you breathe, remember to breath in and out through your nose. For adults, unlike babies, mouth breathing is unhealthy. Mouth breathing in adults usually implies some problem with the nasal passages or sinuses. Never talk while eating. Breathing and digesting are connected together and should be savored and respected, not interrupted by persistent speech. In this way you wull be more sated by smaller more nutritious meaks and avoid unnecessary overeating.

When using the proper breathing technique, inhalation should last twice as long as exhalation. Holding your breath consciously periodically, will help you maximize the delivery of more oxygen to each cell. Your endocrine glands will work better, your heartbeat will be more regular and powerful, your blood will be better saturated with oxygen.

Start now! Let's start practicing some breathing exercises from day one. You may notice some weight loss too! If only 1for 0-15 minutes practise your technique of proper breathing daily, it can and will bring incredible changes. These minutes are well spent and can result in adding more years to your life. Not such a big effort, when such huge dividends result.

Give yourself
enough time to experience nature,
feel its healing effect
and notice the refreshing beauty.
Without experiencing nature,
your body
and then your mind
will become diseased.

Chapter 9

Healthy eating habits

How many times have you heard this common saying - "You are what you eat"? What is true is that what we eat really affects our health, mood, and even happiness. It was the father of modern medicine, Hippocrates who said: "make your food be your cure".

When planning your healthy meals, always remember to make it as much plant-based as possible, and avoid processed food at all costs. It should also be as natural as can be. Food rich in animal proteins like milk, yogurts, cheese or fish should be only an addition to your diet. Meat should be avoided at all costs.

The Macrobiotic diet was popularized in Europe by a Japanese Philosopher – George Oshawa. He based his work on the studies of Far Eastern monks. He wrote over 3000 books promoting a peaceful lifestyle and surrounding oneself with only natural products and materials like cotton and wood. Thanks to this diet, he cured himself of tuberculosis and stayed in good health for many years. Macrobiotic literally means great life (macro – great, bios – life). This diet focuses on locally available food, such as natural wheat, fruits, legumes, and vegetables and does not follow rigid nutritional rules, which is regarded as unnecessary. Followers of the macrobiotic diet completely avoid eating meat, milk or any dairy products.

Macrobiotic diet

The most important component of this particular diet is *whole wheat* which should constitute even half of all daily consumed carbohydrate. It could be, for example, brown rice, various grains, including oatmeal or corn. One meal a day should contain only fresh, naturally grown, cooked vegetables which should contain some leguminous plants like bean, chickpea or peas. The best strategy is to use seasonal vegetables and fruits. If you like soups, you can drink maximally 2 cups a day. Two or three times a week you should eat algae and white fish like cod, flounder, halibut, sole or seabass.

Macrobiotic meals may be prepared by steaming, boiling, roasting in the oven or fried with unrefined oils. Shorter durations of heating are better. When it's cold outside it's good to eat three warm meals. Winter time suggestions are: miso soup, shoyu sauce, olive oil sole.

Beverages should always be prepared using natural or spring water. One should not drink too much, just enough to quench the thirst. Remember if you have certain heart or kidney conditions, too much water may be harmful. Chicory coffee and herbal tea are strongly recommended. You should avoid strong black tea and coffee, sparkling beverages, sodas, and alcohol. Instead of sweats and candies, choose to eat fruits, seeds, and nuts.

The Macrobiotic diet is based on seasons.

In the spring you should eat:
- food that will energize you,
- sprouts, seeds, lightly fermented food, fresh green vegetables,
- lightly cooked or steamed meals.

Summer stands for:
- less caloric or energy filled meals,
- lots of greens, sweet corn, fruits, and pumpkin,
- meals should be mostly steamed or parboiled.

Autumn food is all about:
- food that brings you some energy,
- roots, pumpkin, beans, and wheat.

In the winter is best to eat:
- hot and energizing meals,
- round vegetables, pickled and marinated vegetables, roots,
- a little bit more of fish, olive oil, and salt.

Purification of your body

The internal state of our organs is reflected also in your appearance. Your health depends on the working condition of your intestines, because this is where all the nutrients are absorbed by your body and if we are not careful toxins also. An average adult produces 16-30 pounds of fecaliths in the intestines. Undigested food can produce toxins and carcinogenic substances, which can either cause tumors locally or spread throughout the whole body and settle remotely to create disease. An unavoidable conclusion is that these processes can lead sooner or later to either health or disease depending on our choices.

By recurrently indulging in a harmful diet we can create the perfect environment for diseases to appear and grow. metabolic products inside the body produce toxins that can damage your organs. Intuitively therefore, a set of "clean" intestines means a healthier body.

There are so many different methods of detoxification. Intermittent fasting is one of them. You can find many kinds of different fasts. Some of them are very strict, and while they are quick and effective, need to be carefully monitored. These kinds of fasts completely forbid eating solids. Diet is limited only to water and herbs. Other liquid diets are based on vegetable juices. The mildest liquid diets are based on fruit juices. The length of the fast depends on many factors like the condition and overall health state of the patient, season (longer fasting in the summer, shorter in the winter).

Balanced diet

It's very important to remember to use a proper and balanced diet. Even a high-quality food, eaten in wrong proportions may cause deterioration of your body via metabolic toxins.

Did you know, that it's totally wrong to mix together energizing and "building" kinds of food. On the other hand, you should mix them both with food that supports and builds your immunity.

Let's make it easier to understand with some explanation. Energizing food is obviously everything that is sweet, but certain sour food and all the grains offer energy as well. For example – honey, maple syrup, potatoes, peas, beans, corn, rice, etc...

Food is also a building material for your body. In this building category, you have mostly proteins, obtained from nuts, legume, dairy products, fish and meat.

What kind of food can support your immunity? All the non-starchy vegetables – carrots, beets, brussels sprouts, cauliflower, chicory, salad, broccoli, onion, garlic, bell pepper, cucumbers, green beans, reddish. We can also add in here some vegetable oils.

Three rules for a healthy diet:

1. Never mix carbs with proteins.

Carbs:	Vegetables:	Proteins:
Bread, rolls, rice, cereal, all the flour based products. Digestion of these foods takes 1 to 3 hours.	If blanched, it takes around 2 hours to digest. Up to 4 hours for raw ones.	Meat, fish, legume, beans, nuts, eggs, seafood, dairy products. Digestion of these foods takes from 5 to 7 hours.

Please note the importance of eating each food in the proper order. First carbs, then vegetables, and proteins at the end. If you don't feel like eating proteins, try again after 1-2 hours, when you feel hungry again. Remember – try not to mix more than two kinds of proteins in one meal.

2. Don't drink during meals

Last drink before eating should be at least 30 minutes earlier. Don't drink while eating and 2 hours after eating if you can avoid it. What to drink then? Herbal or fruit tea made from brier, hibiscus, cherry, berries, chokeberry, raspberries etc.

3. Don't mix fruits with anything

Fruits should be eaten on an empty stomach – which doesn't mean only in the morning, but also between meals or as snacks. Most fruits will be tasty blanched with a little bit of ginger, cardamom, and cloves. You can add some dried fruits. After blanching add a little bit of linen oil. At the end add some seed – a different kind every day to augment the nutritional intake of omega 3 fatty acids.

How to change your wrong eating habits:

1. Never mix fat and sour foods together.
2. Don't treat fruit as a dessert.
3. Try to avoid mixing meat with dairy.
4. Don't mix potatoes, rice, and groats (the hulled kernels of various cereal grains, such as oat, wheat, rye, and barley. Groats are whole grains that include the cereal germ and fiber-rich bran portion of the grain).
5. Never drink during a meal.
6. After a warm meal, never drink cold beverages.
7. Try not to eat too much. Finish the meal before you feel full – it doesn't mean you're going to starve yourself!
8. Try to eat cooked and blanched vegetables. Remember to carefully chew the raw ones.
9. Don't eat between the meals.
10. Never mix fruits with milk.
11. If you like tea – drink it 30 minutes before the meal or after it.
12. Don't eat when you don't feel like it, or you don't like the food that was served.
13. Try to eat as many warm meals as possible – especially in the morning.
14. Don't be afraid of fat, if your doctor hasn't forbidden you - your body needs it.
15. Don't mix greasy foods with carbohydrates.
16. **Eat only, when you feel hungry.**
17. Don't try to follow one and the same diet forever – the diet has to be a flexible choice depending on your bodily needs at the time. No diet is perfect for everyone.

Rules for people with fast metabolism

People with faster metabolism need less time to absorb and use nutrients to produce energy. Sometimes that may cause issues with keeping the high energy level all day long. These people are often more capable of snacking between the meals. Snacking healthily between meals can prevent binge overeating and eating the wrong foods between meals.

How to recognize a fast metabolism? Here are some pointers:
- a little increased body temperature,
- hyperactivity,
- high blood pressure,
- easy sweating with effort or temperature rise,
- gaining body weight, especially around arms and shoulders.

It's important to personalize the number of needed nutrients in a diet. Faster metabolism can lead to certain kinds of stress, irritation, weakening of the immune system, and tiredness.

10 important facts about nutrition you should know:

1. Diet rich with saturated fats, refined carbohydrates, and salt may increase the possibility of high blood pressure, diabetes, heart and vascular diseases.

2. Approximately 30% of cancer may be prevented only by following the right diet. Diet rich with fiber and whole grains, that minimizes the amount of fats (particularly animal fat) may lower the chances of many kinds of cancer.

3. Diet with a high amount of fat, sugar, and salt cause an increase in body weight, and, as a result – obesity. Overweight is leading to many heart issues, diabetes, and cancer. What is more, it invariably promotes the feeling of exhaustion, low self-esteem, and poor physical and mental state. Obese people are not necessarily happy people either.

4. Unhealthy diets can affect your mind, altering emotions and mentation, even leading to depression or intensifying the symptoms of PMS, fears, anxiety, and compulsive eating.

5. Processed food with too many artificial ingredients, preservatives, and refined sugar may be one reason for problems with concentration, over-anxiety, irritation, and even aggression. Low levels of essential nutrients in processed food, e.g. chromium can lead to disease: chromium levels are crucial to control blood sugar levels. Processed foods can also play a role in the development of inflammatory bowel disease, also known as Crohn's disease or ulcerative colitis. This time, the culprit is a type of chemical additive called emulsifiers, which are used to extend shelf life and help hold the shape or texture of foods.

6. Not supplying the body with enough calcium (one of the most ba-
   sics nutrients, necessary for the strength and functioning of our
   skeleton) may increase the risk of osteoporosis and fractures.

7. Diet with a low amount of most basic nutrients is very unhealthy
   for the liver. This organ is an important part of the digestive process and it helps the gut to absorb vitamins essential fats and
   minerals. You cannot be healthy if your liver is struggling also. If
   your diet is heavy in saturated fats and alcohol it can lead to serious liver diseases and even cirrhosis or liver failure. Liver disease
   can also affect your kidneys.

8. Eating too much sugar may finally lead to a high level of blood
   sugar and diabetes. Warning symptoms of diabetes include constant thirst, frequent need of urination, problems with vision, exhaustion, and weakening of immunity.

9. Diets with inadequate nutritional elements can seriously weaken
   the immune system. The ability of the immune system to protect
   your body's function against from outside factors such as infections, internal cancer, and inflammatory or auto-immune diseases
   would greatly decrease . Yet another reason to care about a properly balanced diet.

10. Remember to stay strong and resilient in avoiding over-eating, and
    unhealthy eating behaviors!

So, what should we try to eat? Here you have a few useful tips:

1. Drink warm water every morning.
Warm water consumed on an empty stomach helps your digestive system and organs and to elute and flush out all the unneeded by-products of the previous days' food.

2. Flush, hydrate, but don't not flood yourself.
Your stomach doesn't need a lot of water at once. When you're drinking during a meal, you're diluting the gastric acid – this can leading to the less efficient digestion. That is why it's so important to drink at least 30 minutes before and after a meal.

3. Chew carefully.
Always chew slowly and carefully. Savor every bite, don't rush. Try to feel the texture and flavor of every piece of food you're eating. The digestive process starts in your mouth, by biting and mixing food with saliva. This process then activates the rest of your intestinal tract. The better the first step is done, the easier the whole process will proceed. Precisely the way to maximize the amount of absorbed health-giving nutrients. Eating slowly with deliberation and enjoyment promotes satiety and enjoyment of food and prevent rapid over-eating, bloating or indigestion.

4. Eat in peace.
Your body is not able to digest properly when you're nervous, stressed or in a big rush. If you need to, take a few minutes before the meal to relax, slow down and prepare your body for it. Eating should be savored as a peaceful and happy moment in our lives.

5. Not too hot, not too cold.

The temperature of your food matters. The food temperature affects every organ in the digestive track. Ice cold beverages are detrimental to digestion. Excessively hot food isn't any better – heat can burn the mucosa in your mouth or stomach. Did you know that burning your tongue causes a slow loss in the function of your taste buds? Ideally, food is best taken at room temperature – not too cold, but also not too hot.

6. Decorate your plate.

When you see your food, smell it or even think about it, your brain is immediately sending the signals to your salivary glands to start producing saliva. By making food that looks, taste, and smells attractive, you are already stimulating the processes that make your digestion more effective.

7. Read the signals from your body.

It's important to keep in mind, what you really feel like eating. If you are really crave eating something – eat it! Maybe your body is trying to tell you that it needs nutrients that are contained in this particular product. Of course, this doesn't promote gorging on cookies, candies, and snacks. It's more about fruits and vegetables or herbs. Let your body and mind guide you in the store. Does something look good, it feels or smells nice? Get it!

8. Remember breakfast—it may well bethe most important meal of the day.

Always eat a healthy and sufficient breakfast. Morning is a time when your digestion has most of its power. Your whole digestive tract is ready to work. If you skip your morning meal frequently, your energy levels can sag early in the day, so maintain a diet of balanced small frequent healthy meals can be important for weight control and appetite control also. You don't have to eat an enormous breakfast. Just make sure it's nutritious – a fresh fruit, oatmeal or porridge.

9. Don't eat at night.
Your last meal you should eat around two hours before going to bed. Eating too late, can stress your digestive system. If you go to sleep with your stomach full – proper digestion and absorption of the food is impaired. Eating late at night can lead to several health hazards like increase in blood sugar levels, heart diseases, obesity and acidity. Basically, the later you eat, the less your body is prepared to sleep, which can also have adverse effects on your memory and efficiency for the next day.

10. Take care of your kidneys
The kidneys are extremely important organs, crucial for your vitality. At the end of the day take a minute for a little massage. Put your hands on your back, below the waist but above your buttocks. Imagine the warmth and light coming out of your hands. This is how to impart some energy by mindful thinking. Then, massage the area. Drink adequate fluids-stay hydrated.

11. Go to bed earlier
Get adequate sleep which can vary between 6-8 hours a night for most people. The more often you sleep well, the better you would feel the next day. Going to sleep around 11 is already too late – your body's healing and purification processes will be ineffective, and you will feel tired and apathetic.

12. Just be.
Take 5 minutes every day to "just exist mindfully". Take your time to calm down, slow down and step away for a moment from your busy life and all the hectic rush. Don't think too much, just be, and let it be. Close your eyes and focus on your body. These 5 minutes will help you keep your harmony for the rest of the day.

Analysis of some essential elements and nutrients

Nutrient	Source
Calcium	milk, cheese, egg yolk, shellfish, chocolate, figs, peas, beans, yogurt,
Phosphorus	dairy, meat, fish, nuts, legumes,
Iron	meat, shellfish, egg yolks, legumes, nuts, wheat, mushrooms, seeds,
Iodine	iodised salt, seafood, cod-liver oil,
Copper	eggs, wholegrain flour, bean, beets, tomatoes, spinach, asparagus,
Sodium	salt, fish, cheese,
Potassium	legumes, nuts, all vegetables and fruits,
Magnesium	legumes, whole grain products, green vegetables, nuts, apricots, figs, bananas, cocoa,

Sulfur	beef, lamb, fish, chicken, eggs, cheese, beans,
Zinc	meat, fish, oyster, eggs, yeast, vegetables, sunflower and pumpkin seeds,
Selenium	garlic, molasses, salt, nuts, corn, peas, sunflower seeds,
Manganese	seeds, nuts, salads, tea,
Cobalt	beets,
Chromium	yeast, broccoli, grape juice, seafood,
Molybdenum	yeast, cauliflower, rice, spinach, legumes,

For over 30 years now, all over the world, scientists have been working on testing the benefits of these nutrient elements. The amount of these in the human body may affect the chance of developing disease, and enhance health id utilized properly. Based on this kind of analysis doctors can personalize your diet and pharmaceutical supplementation.

Right ratios and balance of some nutrients

Zink to copper
Zink and copper are both very important for your body. They closely affect the production of sex steroids. The wrong proportion between these two may impact the function of these substances. What may happen? Too much or too little of these sex steroids causes problems. Deficiency of sex steroids may lead to osteoporosis, also symptoms of PMS and menopause.

Iron to copper
Amount of these two metals and their mutual ratio is important to the regulation of red blood cell production. Alteration in the amount (excess or deficiency) or in the relative ratio of these metals may cause anemia, liver disease, musculo-skeletal problems etc...

Iron to cobalt
Cobalt "competes" with iron for access to white blood cells. Low concentration of iron can cause an increase in the amount of organ cobalt, especially in the thyroid. It may affect metabolism, cause diarrhea and heart problems.

Sodium to potassium
This ratio is crucial for the adrenals to work well. The wrong proportion can affect the way the body reacts to stress.

Calcium to iron
The mutual proportion here is crucial for iron metabolism. An inadequate ratio may cause anemia.

Copper to molybdenum
Molybdenum actively interacts with other elements. The two are antagonistic – A wrong proportion between these elements can exacerbate shortage of either of these elements.

Calcium to potassium
The thyroid is an organ that is controlled by the proportion of these two elements. If the ratio is too high, that may affect the work of the thyroid and the production of its hormones.

Calcium to phosphor
Phosphorus is necessary for the process of producing energy in all body cells. Derangements in the relative ratios of copper and phosphorous, and phosphorous depletion can affect metabolism, and cause weakened bone strength, rickets, and even kidney stones. The absorption of these elements is controlled by kidney function, and hormones such as the parathyroid hormone.

Synthesis of minerals

Minerals are the very basic elements of the world around us and ourselves. Nitrogen (N), Oxygen (O), hydrogen (H), and carbon (C) are the building materials of all the organic substances and living organisms. They are the elements of proteins, carbs, fats, and vitamins.

Around 30% of all 140 elements are the crucial materials of a human skeleton and soft tissues. They're also extremely important for most of the body functions like blood clotting, oxygen transfer to cells or activation of biological enzymes and hormones.

We can divide all the elements into 3 groups:
- elements essential for living functions,
- neutral ones – organisms can function with or without them,
- toxic elements – ones having a negative impact on the body.

Macro-elements (minerals) whose concentration in the body fluids and tissues reaches over 1µg/g. Some of these macro-elements are chlorine, phosphor, magnesium, potassium, sodium, and calcium.

Microelements (trace elements) whose concentration in the body is less than 1ug/g. For example, arsenic, chromium, pewter, zinc, fluorine, iodine, cobalt, lithium, manganese, molybdenum, nickel, selenium, vanadium, and iron.

Toxic elements can be elements that are nutritionally beneficial in small quantities and toxic in excessive amount. These are mostly aluminum, mercury, cadmium, and lead. How harmful the elements are is depended on two factors – concentration and dose of the element and how long the organism was exposed to its impact. Immunity and ability to eliminate the unwanted substances is also important here. This in turn depends on the condition of the kidneys, liver and whole digestion tract. If the body is in good health and condition, it may be able to fight back and recover quickly from any harmful impact. Vitamins are often a good support in this kind of action for the body.

Toxic substances often accumulate in the liver, kidneys, and pancreas. They may also accumulate in other body tissues – bones, brain tissues, and hair.

The level of toxic element presence may be easily tested for by analysis of body fluids like blood, urine or cerebrospinal fluid but also directly from tissue samples such as hair or skin. Concentration of many elements is directly depended on the diet and external exposure. Lead poisoning for example can result from drinking water that passes through old lead pipes. Conversely, adverse effects can result from too low levels of these elements and these can be visible in the condition of the hair and nails where metabolism and growth is slowed.

Mineral concentration in the body is depending on many factors – the quality and quantity of food, physical activity, pollution, and water contamination. Its metabolism is regulated by nervous system and hormones. Whole body metabolism and many living functions depend on the amount of these little elements—we should therefore give them attention!

Calcium

Calcium is necessary for many processes in your body. Calcium is crucial for nerve and muscular system function. We recognize that calcium is a necessary building material for the skeleton. It also helps in blood clotting, activation of enzymes, functioning of heart, muscles and nerves. It is an important part of the wound healing process and has anti-allergic functions. The amount of calcium in the body is vastly higher than the amount on any other element.
Calcium also affects your nerves, to control your mood, optimism, motivation, and harmony. We have already emphasized how important harmony is to your health and overall condition.

Calcium Deficiency
The deficit of calcium may result in muscle cramps, numbness and tingling, paint in joints, slower pulse. After sometime this may develop into more serious problems like heart rhythm disturbances, internal bleeding, sleeping disorder, anxiety and panic attacks, fragile bones, rickets, and osteoporosis.

Dosage: An average adult needs approximately 900mg of calcium a day.

Sodium

Sodium is the most important cation (positively ion) of the body's extracellular fluid. One of its roles is maintaining the right osmotic pressure of body fluids and keeping the body from excessive osmotic loss. Sodium is necessary to keep muscles and cellular tissues in good condition. Sodium and potassium are essential to electrolyte management and acid-base homeostasis. Sodium ions form the basis for transmitting electrical signals along and between nerves.

Excess Sodium
Over-dosage of salt (sodium) may result in high blood pressure, vessels problems, diabetes, kidney, liver and stomach problems, high level of cholesterol, and exhaustion.

Dosage: An adult needs around 575-625mg a day.

Potassium

Potassium is a cellular ion controlling the right hydro-electrolytes homeostasis. It's crucial for the functioning of nerve and muscular systems.
It's the most important cation of extracellular fluid. It's also extremely important for the heart. It has many roles for human metabolism, for example biosynthesis of proteins. Together with sodium, it controls the electrolytes and acid-base homeostasis. It takes its role in transmitting the stimulates. It's affecting the right functioning of many organs like brain, heart, and muscles.

Potassium Deficiency
To low amount of potassium in the body would result in problems with digestion track – diarrhea or vomiting, kidney, liver and stomach issues or diabetes. Depletion of potassium may appear with many symptoms: headaches, muscles pain, dry skin, over irritation, fainting, sleeping disorder, stomach cramps, acne, long time of wound healing, heartbeat issues, exhaustion, problems with concentration, long reaction time, constipation.

Dosage: An average adult needs approximately 3500 mg of potassium a day.

Phosphor

Phosphor is present in every single cell of the human body. However, over 80% of the phosphor appearing in bones, occurs together with calcium. It is important for storing and transmission of energy. The right ratio between phosphor and calcium affects the absorption and digestion of other elements and the building process of teeth, bones, acid-base homeostasis, brain and nerve cells. Calcium and phosphorous also regulate and participate in the synthesis of our body's building blocks the nucleic acids present in DNA and RNA.

Phosphorous Shortage
This can result in anemia, depletion of calcium in the bones, breathing problems, exhaustion, and nervous system disorders.

Dosage: Daily dosage for an adult is about 700-900mg.

Zinc

Zinc has a basic role for many living functions. As an element of many enzymes, it takes place in the metabolism of proteins and carbs. This is very important for the reproductive system, especially for men, and the process of metabolic detoxification. It also prevents the body from absorption of excessive amounts of toxic metals.
Crucial for the synthesis of proteins, metabolism, and bodily immunity, zinc lays a role in keeping the homeostasis of other elements like manganese, selenium, and copper.

Shortage
Shortage of zinc may result in: nyctalopia (inability to see in dim light), low appetite, lack of motivation, skin rash, shaking of hands, breakable nails, loss of hair, aging, weak immunity, dry eyes, depression, movement and walking problems, disability of taste, exhaustion, growing disorder, diabetes. Shortage of this element can also worsen the amount of skin wrinkles. Zinc deficiency also affects the production of hormones and enzymes.

Zinc Excess
An overdose of zinc is toxic for your body. Common symptoms here are anemia and vomiting. Zinc poisoning is mostly the effect of eating some fruits and vegetables that were sprayed with some zinc-based chemicals or stored in zinc containing containers.

Average Dosage: 15 mg/day for an adult.

Magnesium

Magnesium is an important element of human metabolism. It plays its role in cardiac and skeletal muscles contractions, and in case of the heart, it helps maintain a regular heartbeat. Magnesium is needed for the blood clotting process and stabilization of the blood cells. It affects the immune system, helping in the development of the skeleton. Magnesium has a well-known role for promoting concentration and learning processes, relaxation and fighting anxiety, headaches and dizziness. It is necessary for absorption and synthesis of proteins, sugars, calcium, vitamin C, sodium, and potassium. So, it can be very useful in the therapy of nervous problems and depression.

Magnesium Shortage
Shortage of magnesium would result in shaking and cramps of muscles, anemia, nausea, vomiting, heartbeat disorders, depression, over irritation, anxiety, hallucinations, and sleeping disorders.

Dosage: Daily dosage for an adult is approximately 300mg, and is useful in individuals with high level of stress, excess alcohol use, or intense physical activity. It is also supplemented in those taking diuretics which cause its loss.

Iron

Iron is a structural element of many body enzymes and participates control the oxidation-reduction process in the body cells. Iron is a basic part of hemoglobin, myoglobin, and many different enzymes needed for cellular respiration. Iron is necessary for the appropriate function of the stomach, liver, and many different organs. It controls enzymes, blood cells, cellular respiration, synthesis of hormones, growth of muscle tissues, heart, and immune system. It also affects the absorption and function of other elements, especially the functionally antagonistic ones, like cadmium, manganese, lead, and zinc.

Iron Shortage
Results of iron shortage are anemia, dyspnea, issues of metabolism and digestion, damage of tissues, exhaustion, and even the disorders in children psychological growth.

Dosage: An average adult needs 10-18mg of iron a day.

Copper

Copper is one of the most basic elements of human blood. Its concentration should vary around 100-130 mg per 100ml of blood, and is higher for women than men. It is no surprise that copper is necessary for the healthy functioning of the circulation. It is also important for the nervous system and regeneration of tissues. Copper supports cellular regeneration in response to the damaging actions of reactive oxygen species. It activates body enzymes, and assists in the absorption and metabolism of iron. Copper also supports the brain cell function.

Iron Shortage
Shortage of copper results in anemia, issues with growth and reproduction, migraines, blood circular system, and cellular respiration problems.

Dosage: Average daily dosage is around 1.5-4mg.

Manganese

Manganese plays a part in many physiological processes, as an activator and regulator of metabolism, especially that of glucose, carbohydrates, and proteins. It's also one of the elements of enzymes but it's not necessary and can be replaced by another element, for example, magnesium. It's an important element of bones, nervous system, and metabolism of some vitamins. It supports the blood clotting and regeneration of tissues. As a catalyst, it helps with digestion of fats and cholesterol. There are many functions and actions that depend on manganese: sexual activity, hair coloring, enzyme function, cellular respiration, correct blood sugar level, hormone production. Manganese helps to prevent bone deformation and fracture and supports the coordination of body movement.

Manganese Deficiency
Inadequate amounts of body manganese can result in painful joints, low libido, pessimism, hearing problems, dry skin, weight loss, exhaustion, vision problems, diabetes, dizziness.

Dosage: 2.5 - 6 mg/day for an average adult.

Selenium

Selenium is one of the most important micro-elements and it must be provided within the diet. You can find it in wheat, eggs meat, diary, and shellfish. We need to realize that not every kind of selenium is easy to absorb or good for our body. The best source of selenium is from yeast. To absorb selenium will require proteins and vitamins. Selenium is important to preventing cellular aging and supporting the enzymatic system. It also protects the cells and tissues from damage caused by reactive oxygen species ("oxidative stress"). Selenium enhances the immune system and thyroid function. It can lower the chances of rheumatic and other joints disease. For men, selenium is important for prostatic health, and to enhance libido and sexual activity.
Selenium may even be able to retard the development of prostate cancer!

Selenium Deficiency
The symptoms of selenium shortage are pale skin, muscle and joint pain, breakable nails, fast aging, weak immunity, heartbeat issues, and vision problems.

Dosage: Average daily dosage is around 60ug for women and 70μg for men.

Recommended supplementary literature

Campbell T. Colin i Campbell II Thomas M., *Nowoczesne zasady odżywiania*,
Wyd. Galaktyka, Łódź 2011.
Celma AlexRovira, Trias de Bes Fernando, *Szczęście czy fart?*
Wyd. Amber, 2004.
Dobroń Grażyna, *Instrukcja samoobsługi człowieka*, Wyd. Czarna Owca Warszawa, 2010.
Pinkola Estes Clarissa, *Biegnąca z wilkami*, Wyd. Zysk i S-ka, Poznań 2001.
Exel Wolfgang, Dungl Willi, *Naturalne metody lecznicze*, Świat Książki, Warszawa 1995.
Gajer Paweł, *Radość Życia*, 2013.
Janus Ewa, *Bądź aniołem swojego życia*, Wyd. Rawi, 2003.
Janus Andrzej, *Postawiłem na zdrowie,* Wyd. Biosłone, 2006.
Małachow Gienadij, *Samoleczenie i uzdrawianie,* Wyd. ABA.
McKeith Gillian, *Jesteś tym, co jesz,* Dom Wydawniczy Rebis Poznań.
Mindell Dr Arnold, *Siła Ciszy,* Wyd. Kos, Katowice 2007.
Morrison,Ayurveda Judith H., *Co robić, by czuć się dobrze,* Wyd. Delta.
Ornish Dean, *Miłość i przetrwanie*, Wyd. Jacek Santorski&CO, Warszawa 1998.
Pomorski Marian, *Długowieczność zależy od ciebie*, Wyd. Marpo Kielce 1997.
Roach Gesze Michael, *Diamentowe ostrze,* Wyd. Czerwony Słoń, Gdańsk 2000.
Schache Ruediger, *Magnetyzm serca*, Wyd. Sonia Draga, Katowice 2009.
Schwartz David J., *Pozytywne myślenie drogą do sukcesu,* Wyd. Bertelsman Media, Warszawa 2000.
Stone Gene, *Sekrety ludzi, którzy nie chorują,* Wyd. Weldbild, Warszawa 2010.
Tombak Michał, *Droga do zdrowia*, Firma Księgarska Serwis, Łódź 2008.
Wasmer Smith Linda, *Psychika i ciało*, Prószyński i S-ka, Warszawa 1998.
Wiśniewska-Roszkowska Kinga, Zgirski-Starość Alojzy, *Metabolizm, Rewitalizacja,* Wyd. Państwowy Zakład Wydawnictw Lekarskich, Warszawa 1973.
Wiśniewska-Roszkowska Kinga, *Rewitalizacja i długowieczność,* Wyd. Różdżkarz, Poznań 1990.

Table of Contents

www.ingramcontent.com/pod-product-compliance
Lightning Source LLC
LaVergne TN
LVHW010343200726
843507LV00010B/1625